A PLACE FOR
FISH

For Doug, who loves to fish
but respects his catch
—M. S.

In memory of my sister, Fareedah Muhammad,
and my father, Henry Drew Higgins, who taught
me about the great places for fish in Arkansas
—H. B.

Ω

Published by
PEACHTREE PUBLISHERS
1700 Chattahoochee Avenue
Atlanta, Georgia 30318-2112

www.peachtree-online.com

Book design by Loraine M. Joyner
Composition by Maureen Withee
Illustrations created in acrylic on cold press illustration board.
Title typeset in Hardlyworthit; main text typeset in Monotype's Century
Schoolbook with Optima initial capitals. Sidebars typeset in Optima.

Printed and manufactured in Singapore
10 9 8 7 6 5 4 3 2 1
First Edition

Library of Congress Cataloging-in-Publication Data
Stewart, Melissa.
  A place for fish / written by Melissa Stewart ; illustrated by
Higgins Bond. -- 1st ed.
    p. cm.
  ISBN 13: 978-1-56145-562-1 / ISBN 10: 1-56145-562-8
  1. Rare fishes--Juvenile literature. 2. Fishes--Effect of human beings on-
-Juvenile literature. 3. Fishes--Ecology--Juvenile literature. I. Bond,
Higgins, ill. II. Title.
  QL617.7.S74 2011
  597.17--dc22
                                              2010026689

A PLACE FOR

FISH

Written by
Melissa Stewart

Illustrated by
Higgins Bond

PEACHTREE
ATLANTA

Fish make our world a better place. But sometimes people do things that make it hard for them to live and grow.

If we work together to help these special creatures, there will always be a place for fish.

ON THE MOVE

A fish swims by bending its body from side to side. Its strong tail pushes it forward through the water. Paired fins on its sides help it start, stop, and turn. Top and bottom fins help a fish keep its balance. Fish with slim fins and a narrow tail can swim fast. Fish with large, wide fins and a square tail swim slowly, but they can turn quickly.

masked angelfish

For fish to survive, they need to stay safe and healthy.
Many sharks die when they accidentally get trapped in fishing nets.

When scientists learn where sharks live and people agree not to fish in those places, sharks can live and grow.

HAMMERHEAD SHARK

Sharks have lived on Earth for 450 million years. But now they are in danger of disappearing forever. Each year, thousands of hammerhead sharks are killed by nets set out to catch tuna and swordfish.

Scientists recently discovered that hammerheads migrate along set paths at specific times of the year. They asked fishing crews to avoid those areas while sharks migrate, so now sharks have a better chance of surviving.

Some fish are harmed by the chemicals power plants produce when they burn coal to make electricity.

NORTHERN PIKE

As power plants burn coal to make electricity, they pump out smoke full of chemicals. The chemicals mix with clouds to produce acid rain. When the acid rain comes into contact with rocks at the bottom of a lake, the rocks release a material that damages fish gills. How can we help save northern pikes and other fish? By conserving electricity and using solar power and wind power in more homes and businesses.

a wind farm

When people find other ways to make electricity, fish can live and grow.

Some fish have trouble surviving when farmers use chemicals to make crops grow bigger and stronger.

When farmers and scientists find new ways to improve crops, fish can live and grow.

LINED SEAHORSE

The land surrounding the Chesapeake Bay has rich soil. In the 1960s, farmers in the area began using powerful fertilizers to make their plants grow better. When the chemicals drained into the bay, algae grew quickly and used most of the oxygen in the water. That made it hard for lined seahorses and other fish to survive. Since 2003, farmers and citizens have worked together to reduce the amount of fertilizer entering the bay. Can lined seahorses make a comeback? Scientists are waiting to find out.

S ome fish are so beautiful that people like to keep them as pets.

YELLOW TANG

Each year, divers collect more than 200,000 yellow tangs from Hawaii's coral reefs. They know that people with home aquariums will pay a lot of money for the colorful fish. Because the number of yellow tangs has fallen 47 percent since 2000, scientists are trying to raise the fish in their labs to sell to the public. If they succeed, divers will have no good reason to remove wild yellow tangs from the ocean.

yellow tang

When people stop catching these colorful creatures,
fish can live and grow.

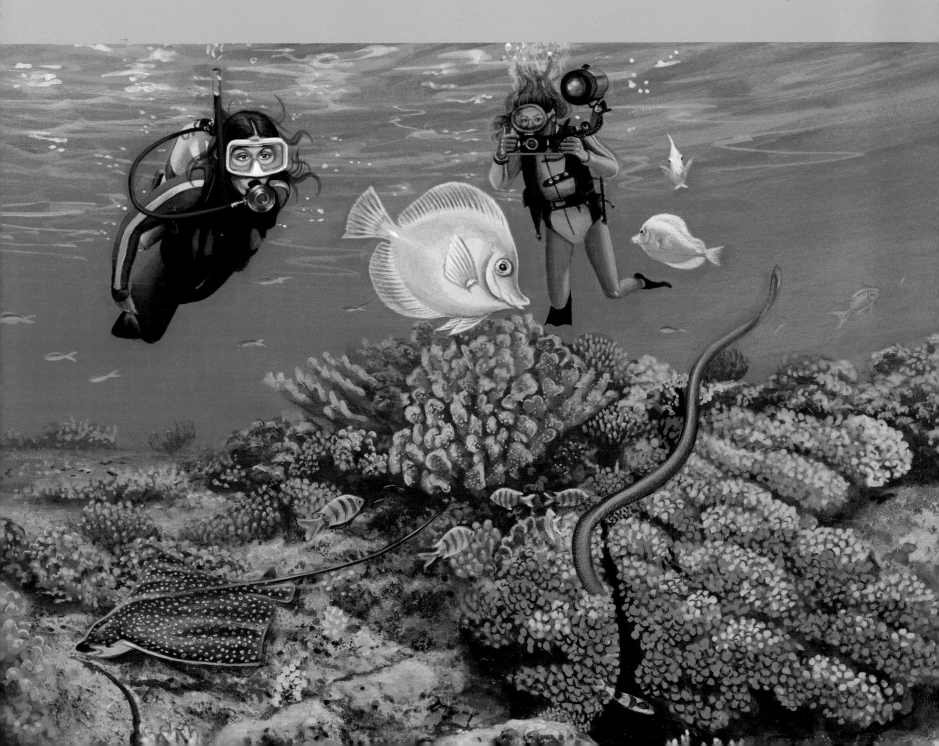

Some fish have unusual body parts that people like to collect.

When laws stop people from selling the special body parts, fish can live and grow.

SMALLTOOTH SAWFISH

For centuries, healers in Asia added sawfish fins to their remedies because they thought the fins had magical powers. And people all over the world liked to collect the sawfish's long, toothy snout. By 1997, there were almost no sawfish left. Today, it's against the law to catch or sell any part of a sawfish in the United States. The fish is still in danger, but scientists hope it will be able to survive.

SMALLMOUTH BASS

Many people buy young goldfish as pets. But when the fish outgrow their tank, their owners may decide to dump them in a local pond. Goldfish eat smaller native fish such as smallmouth bass and their eggs. And as goldfish feed, they destroy bass nests by stirring up mud and sand. People should never release a goldfish in a natural body of water.

smallmouth bass

When people stop dumping pet goldfish into local waters,
native fish can live and grow.

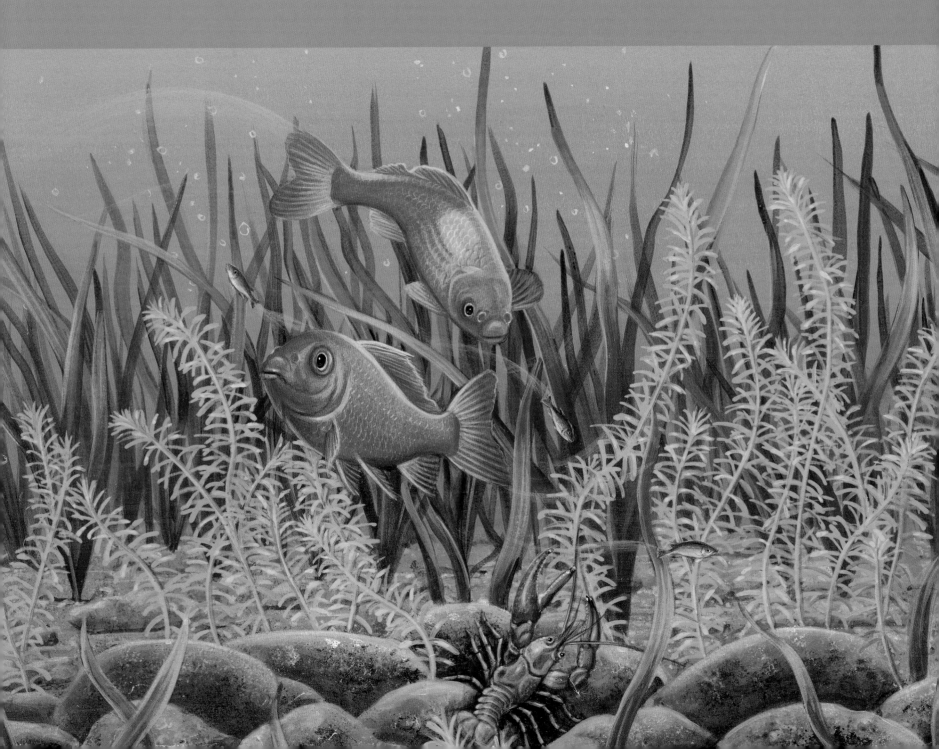

*S*ome fish taste so delicious that people catch and eat too many of them.

NORTH ATLANTIC SWORDFISH

At one time, millions of swordfish lived along the Atlantic coast of North America. But by the 1990s, scientists realized the swordfish were in danger of disappearing forever. The U.S. government passed a law making it illegal to fish in the places where swordfish lay their eggs. Chefs across North America agreed to take swordfish off their menus. By 2006, the swordfish population had made an amazing comeback.

When scientists, chefs, and lawmakers work together,
fish can live and grow.

Fish also have trouble surviving when their natural homes
are destroyed. Some fish can only live near coral reefs.

When people work to protect coral reefs, fish can live and grow.

SPOTTED TRUNKFISH

The spotted trunkfish depends on Florida's coral reefs for food and shelter. But these reefs face many dangers. Chemicals in household cleaners make coral animals weak, so they can't fight diseases. Boats sometimes bump into and destroy reefs that have taken hundreds of years to form. To help solve the problem, Florida's Coral Reef Conservation Program is teaching people simple ways to protect coral reefs and the fish that depend on them.

spotted trunkfish

S ometimes farmers drain water from rivers and lakes so their animals will have enough to drink. But that can make it hard for fish to survive.

LAHONTAN
CUTTHROAT TROUT

Farmers have been draining water from the rivers and streams that feed Walker Lake in Nevada for more than a hundred years. Over time, the level of the lake has fallen 140 feet. Because the shallow water warms up quickly and contains a lot of salt, the lake is no longer a good home for Lahontan cutthroat trout. But farmers and scientists are working together to find ways to conserve water, so the future looks bright for the lake and the fish.

When farmers find ways to use less water, fish can live and grow.

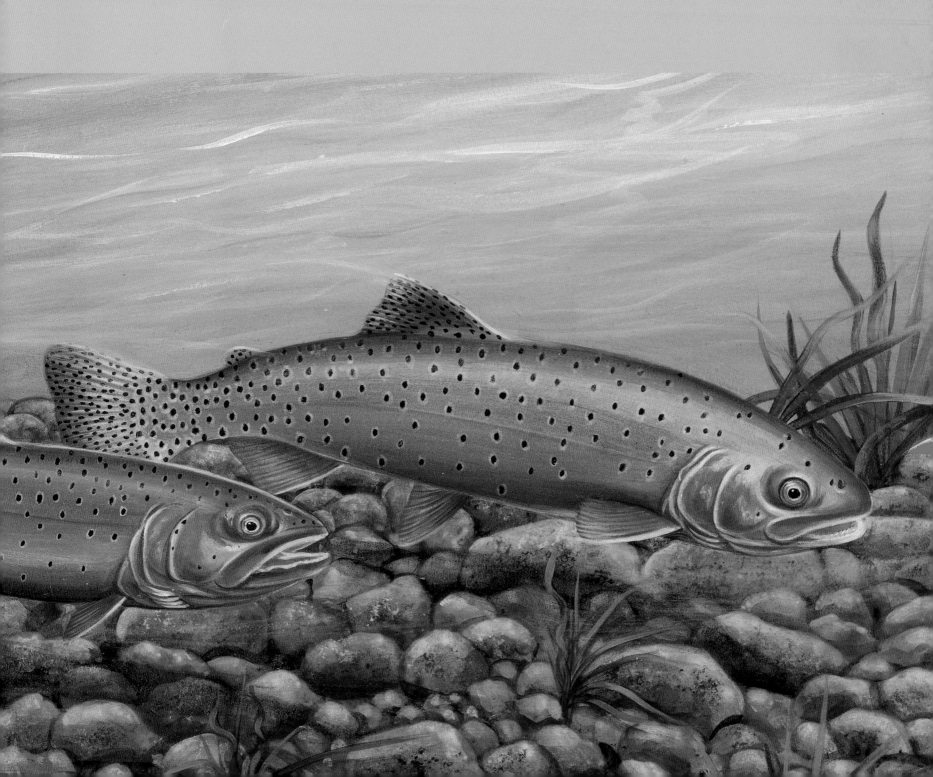

W hen workers build roads through forests and cut down trees, dirt washes into nearby streams. Sand and soil fills in spaces between rocks where fish hide from enemies.

When people work to protect natural places, fish can live and grow.

ATLANTIC SALMON

In the 1990s, logging companies built roads through the forests near Lake Branch in Quebec, Canada, and cut down hundreds of trees. Tons of soil eroded into nearby streams. As the sediments spread over the streams' rocky bottoms, salmon had to move into the open water. That made it easy for predators to catch them. Soon, the salmon were almost gone. But then a group of caring citizens convinced the loggers to change how they operate, so they would cause less erosion. By 2000, the salmon population was recovering.

RAINBOW TROUT

In 1968, workers built a dam across Mt. Scott Creek in Happy Valley, Oregon. The dam made it difficult for rainbow trout to swim upstream and lay their eggs. It also blocked young fish from swimming downstream. Many of the fish living in Mt. Scott Creek and nearby streams died. In 2002, workers removed the dam. Now the fish are making a comeback.

rainbow trout

We build dams to control the flow of water along rivers and streams. But the dams make it hard for fish to swim from place to place.

When people remove dams, fish can live and grow.

When too many fish die, other living things may also struggle to survive.

WE NEED FISH

Fish help us survive. People living in the United States eat about 6 billion pounds of fish every year. Fish is an important source of protein. About 45 million people all over the world make a living catching or processing fish.

That's why it's so important to protect fish and the places where they live.

OTHER ANIMALS NEED FISH

Fish are an important part of the food chain. Fish eggs are good sources of food for turtles and for other fish. Adult fish are eaten by bears, raccoons, muskrats, otters, seals, bats, and birds. Without fish, many other creatures would go hungry.

F ish have lived on Earth for more than 450 million years. Sometimes people do things that can harm fish.

But there are many ways you can help these special creatures live far into the future.

HELPING FISH

❖ If you catch a small fish, let it go.

❖ Always wash fishing gear thoroughly before using it in another body of water. This will help prevent invasive species from spreading.

❖ Do not throw trash into any body of water.

❖ Do not pour household cleaners or other chemicals down the drain.

❖ Conserve water. Don't let it run while you brush your teeth. Take showers instead of baths. Collect rainwater and use it to water plants.

❖ Join a group of people working to protect or restore rivers, lakes, streams, ponds, or ocean areas near your home.

FASCINATING FISH FACTS

No one knows exactly how many kinds of fish live on Earth. So far, scientists have discovered more than 25,000 different species. Some researchers think there may 15,000 more species left to identify.

Most fish swim in groups called schools, but a group of seahorses is called a herd.

The stout infantfish is the smallest fish on Earth. It could easily sit on top of a pencil eraser. The great whale shark is the world's largest fish. It is larger than a school bus.

Fish don't have eyelids, so they can't close their eyes and fall asleep like we do. Most fish rest quietly during the night, but some fish are almost always on the move.

Does the idea of kissing a fish make your skin crawl?
Then consider this: Most brands of lipstick contain ground-up fish scales.

Most young fish are called fingerlings, but young sharks and sawfish are called pups.

Acknowledgments

The author wishes to thank Doug Stewart, wetland scientist and principal at Stantec Consulting,
for his help in preparing this manuscript.

Selected Bibliography

BOOKS AND ARTICLES

Burr, Brooks M. and Lawrence M. Page. A Field Guide to Freshwater Fishes: North America North of Mexico. Boston: Houghton Mifflin, 1991.

National Audubon Society. Field Guide to North American Fishes. New York: Knopf, 2002.

* Parker, Steve. Fish. New York: Knopf, 2005.

* Sayre, April Pulley. Trout Are Made of Trees. Watertown, MA: Charlesbidge, 2008.

* Sayre, April Pulley. Trout, Trout, Trout: A Fish Chant. Minnetonka, MN: NorthWord, 2003.

Schultz, Ken. Field Guide to Saltwater Fish. New York: Wiley, 2003.

WEBSITES

Fish

* http://animals.nationalgeographic.com/animals/fish/

Fish Videos

* http://www.kidport.com/reflib/science/Videos/Animals/Fish/FishVideoIndex.htm#Menu

Secrets of the Seahorse

* http://aquarium.ucsd.edu/Education/Learning_Resources/Secrets_of_the_Seahorse/

*Recommended resources for young explorers

☐ RANGE

MASKED ANGELFISH

Hawaii

☐ RANGE

HAMMERHEAD SHARK

☐ RANGE

NORTHERN PIKE

☐ RANGE

LINED SEAHORSE

THE BAHAMAS

☐ RANGE

YELLOW TANG

Hawaii

☐ RANGE

SMALLTOOTH SAWFISH

All range boundaries are approximate.